HISTORY SHOWTIME

ROMANS

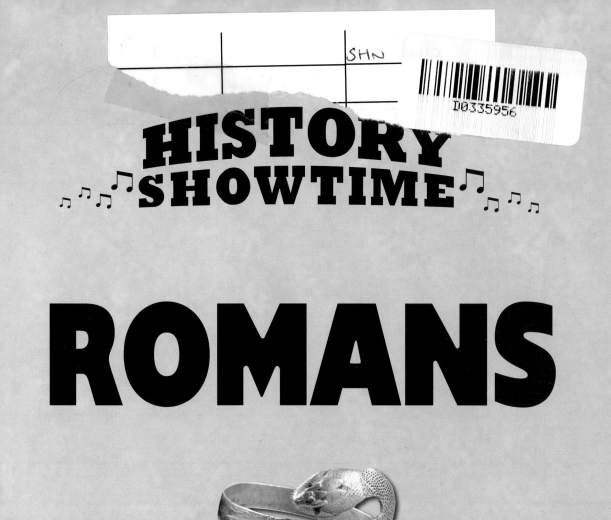

Liza Phipps & Avril Thompson

W
FRANKLIN WATTS

About this book

History Showtime takes an interactive approach to learning history. Alongside the key information about an ancient civilisation are songs for children to perform, crafts to make and games to play. These are brought together at the end of the book by a play about a big event or aspect of the history of the civilisation which children can perform themselves, using the crafts they have made over the course of the book as props and including performances of the songs the children have learned.

These icons signpost the different activities:

Crafts   Games   Songs   Playscript

To enrich the learning experience, music from the book is also available to download online as audio tracks, music scores and lyrics. Visit www.franklinwatts.co.uk/historyshowtime or just scan:

This logo appears where downloadable material is available.

First published in paperback in Great Britain in 2015 by The Watts Publishing Group

Text, lyrics and music copyright © Liza Phipps and Avril Thompson 2013
Avril Thompson and Liza Phipps have asserted their right to be identified as the Authors of this Work

ISBN: 978 1 4451 1488 0
Library eBook ISBN: 978 1 4451 2532 9
Dewey classification number: 937

A CIP catalogue record for this book is available from the British Library.

Editor: Julia Bird
Designer: Rita Storey

With thanks to our model Samuel Jakeman and to the choir of the Jackie Palmer Stage School, High Wycombe.

Photo acknowledgements: AndreaAstes/istock: 20. Araldo de Luca/Corbis: 17t. The Art Archive/Alamy: 1, 10t, 11t, 12b, 14b, 19m, 29. DEA/G. Dagli Orti: 16b. DurdenImages/istock: 13b, 28. Emicristea/dreamstime: 7b. Erin Babnik/Alamy: 12t. Gors4730/dreamstime: 18bl. INTERFOTO/Alamy: 21b.

JeniFoto/Shutterstock: 4b. Kamira/Shutterstock: 18t. Lebrecht Music & Arts/Corbis: 24b. LUCARELLI TEMISTOCLE/Shutterstock: 23t. mauritius images GmbH/Alamy: 23b. McCarthy's PhotoWorks/Shutterstock: 6b. meunierd/Shutterstock: 6t. mountainpix/Shutterstock: 9m, 10b. Museum of London: 13t. Nancypitman/dreamstime: 19t. Nikreates/Alamy: 21t, 30. nito/Shutterstock: 16t. Orhan Cam/Shutterstock: 24t. Photoman29/Shutterstock: 22t. Regien Paassen/Shutterstock: 7t. Roberto Aquilano/Shutterstock: 22b. Rognar/dreamstime: 18br. Sklifas Steven/Alamy: 9t. Shutterstock: 8b. Snem/dreamstime: 14t. StevanZZ/Shutterstock: 8t. verityjohnson/Shutterstock: 14m. Wikimedia Commons: 27.

Every attempt has been made to clear copyright. Should there be any inadvertent omission, please apply to the publisher for rectification.

Franklin Watts
An imprint of
Hachette Children's Group
Part of The Watts Publishing Group
Carmelite House
50 Victoria Embankment
London EC4Y 0DZ

An Hachette UK Company
www.hachette.co.uk

www.franklinwatts.co.uk

Contents

Words in **bold** can be found in
the glossary on page 31.

The Roman Empire

The city of Rome lies on the River Tiber in the country we now call Italy. It gave its name to one of the biggest and most successful **empires** the world has ever seen.

The Roman Empire stretched from Britannia (now Britain) to Africa.

A great power

The Roman Empire began in around 330 BCE when the Roman army started **conquering** new lands. By 117 CE, the Roman Empire covered most of Europe, the Middle East and North Africa. All of the people living in the empire paid Roman **taxes** and obeyed Roman laws.

The Colosseum, where Ancient Romans watched **gladiators** fight, still stands in Rome today.

Rome

The city of Rome was at the heart of the Roman Empire. The earliest **inhabitants** of Rome were a **tribe** called the Latins. They gave their name to the language which was spoken throughout much of the empire. Rome grew to be a city of one million inhabitants, the largest city in the world at the time. Many of its fine buildings can still be seen today.

Citizens

Roman society was very structured and everybody knew their place in it. Only men could be full Roman **citizens**, which meant that they could vote in **elections** and join the army.

TRUE!

According to **legend**, Rome was founded by twin brothers called Romulus and Remus. They fought over who should be king of Rome. Romulus killed his brother and became king.

Civis Romanus sum

'Civis Romanus sum' means 'I am a Roman citizen' in Latin. Only men who were born in Rome or had been a soldier in the army could be full Roman citizens. Sing this song to show how proud they were to be a citizen of the great Roman Empire.

The Roman army

The Roman army was one of the greatest fighting forces there has ever been. Its job was to conquer new lands for the empire and to keep the peace within it.

Hard life

Its army was very important to the Roman Empire and soldiers were very well trained and equipped. They were also well paid, but it was a tough life. Soldiers were expected to march over 30 kilometres a day, carrying their weapons and a heavy pack, and building roads and bridges as they went. Roman soldiers had to serve at least 25 years in the army. When they retired, they were given a **pension** or a plot of land to farm.

This is how Roman soldiers may have looked as they marched across the empire.

The Roman standard

The army was organised into groups. A legion was made up of about 5,000 soldiers. Smaller groups of about 100 soldiers were called centuries. Each legion marched behind a silver eagle **standard** with the letters SPQR on it. These stood for the Roman **motto** 'senatus populusque Romanus' which means 'The senate and the people of Rome'.

S.P.Q.R.

TIBERIUS CAESAR IMP

LEGIO X

Weapons and armour

A Roman soldier wore armour made of leather and metal plates, and a metal helmet. He carried a heavy cloak that could be used as a blanket. His weapons included a short sword, a dagger, two spears and a heavy shield. When the soldiers were under attack, they locked their shields together over their heads and around them to form the famous 'testudo' or tortoise formation.

The testudo formation was designed to defend Roman soldiers from the enemy's weapons.

Home from home

The Roman army built many impressive **forts** to defend the borders of the empire. Inside they were like small towns. Each contained a hospital, grain stores, bath house and toilets, and **barracks** for the soldiers to live in.

TRUE!

Roman soldiers were not allowed to marry while they were in the army.

The main gate of a Roman fort that still stands in the modern day country of Romania.

Buildings and towns

The Romans were great builders and **engineers**. Many Roman buildings are still in use now, more than 2,000 years after they were constructed.

Brick by brick

The Romans made bricks out of clay, which they baked before use. This made the bricks stronger and more **durable**, and meant that they could be used to build bigger structures than ever before. The Romans also invented concrete, using ash from Italian volcanoes. This allowed them to build complicated structures such as aqueducts to bring fresh running water into towns, and public drains to carry away waste water.

This ancient aqueduct in France was built to bring water to the Roman town of Nîmes.

TRUE!

The Romans invented central heating.

Great towns

The Romans built towns throughout the empire. Most of them followed a plan based on the city of Rome. All Roman towns had walls around them. At the centre of the town was a large open-air meeting place, the forum, which was also the market place. All towns and cities had public baths and toilets, and most of them had an amphitheatre (a large space where public shows took place). There were also temples to gods or goddesses.

The ruins of the forum in the centre of Rome can still be visited today.

Homes

Where people lived depended on whether they were rich or poor. Poorer people usually lived in flats, often just above the shops or workshops where they worked. Wealthy citizens lived in houses nearer the edge of town and would also often have a second home, a farm known as a villa, out in the countryside. These houses were usually comfortably furnished and beautifully decorated with wall paintings and mosaics (see below) on the floor.

This villa, with its garden and shady walkways, belonged to a rich Roman family.

Make a mosaic

Mosaics were used by the Romans as decoration. They were made by setting small pieces of stone or glass into plaster.

This mosaic of an owl dates from Roman times.

1. Sketch your design onto a sheet of paper.

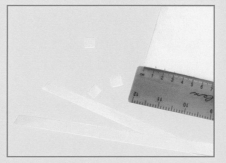

2. Cut different pieces of coloured paper into 1cm strips. Cut the strips into 1cm squares.

3. Glue coloured squares onto the outlines of your design.

4. Glue contrasting coloured squares within the lines to finish the mosaic picture.

At home

The father was the head of every Roman household and everyone, including his wife, had to obey him.

Work

Wealthy men worked as lawyers, government officials, businessmen, army generals or even **senators**. Less wealthy men worked as farmers, shopkeepers or craftsmen, and their wives would also work to help their husbands. Rich women did not go out to work. Instead, they looked after the household and the family's money.

This carving shows a Roman family eating at a banquet.

Slaves

Slaves belonged to their owners and were not paid for their work. They were not Roman citizens and they had no **rights**, but they had to do much of the hard work in a Roman household. Very often they were **prisoners of war** or the children of slaves. Some owners treated their family slaves well and might even give them their freedom after many years of service.

Slaves worked very hard looking after a Roman household. They cooked, cleaned and even helped to dress their owners.

Children

In richer families, boys went to school to learn maths, reading and how to give speeches. Girls were kept at home and although they were sometimes taught to read, write and play a musical instrument, their main purpose was to learn how to run a household and be a good wife. Children of poorer families did not go to school, but were expected to work to help their parents.

Coming of age

When they were born, boys were given a locket called a bulla to protect them. It contained a lucky **charm** and was hung around their neck. Boys became adults at the age of 14 when they gave up their bulla to the household gods. If they were the sons of wealthy citizens, they then also received a **toga** in a special **ceremony**. Girls were often married at the age of 13 or 14.

This gold bulla, found in the ruins of Pompeii (see page 23), would have belonged to a boy from a wealthy family.

Make a bulla

1. Using a compass, draw two circles 5cm in diameter onto a piece of paper.

2. Draw a flap shape, like the one shown top left, onto the side of one of the circles and cut both shapes out. Use the paper shapes as templates to cut out both pieces from a sheet of thin foam or felt.

3. Paint glue around the curved edge of the shape, leaving a small gap. Place the circle on top and leave to dry.

4. Put a coin or charm into the pocket of the bulla and fold the flap over the top.

5. To decorate the bulla, glue braid round the front edge of the pocket. Spray or paint the bulla gold.

6. Glue the flap down and leave to dry. Thread a chain or necklace under the flap. Your bulla is ready to wear!

Fashion and appearance

The Romans took great care with their appearance. Clothes, jewellery and make-up all helped to show whether they were rich or poor.

Clothes

Roman clothing was quite simple. Everybody, rich or poor, citizen or slave, wore a simple **tunic** which was usually made of wool or **linen**. Richer people wore cotton or silk. Over the top of this, wealthy women wore a long dress called a stola. Wealthy men could wear a toga if they were a citizen. The most important men of all, the senators, wore a white toga with a purple stripe along the edge. All Romans wore leather sandals on their feet.

A fashionable young Roman couple.

How to wear a toga

1. A toga was a large semi-circle of cloth. To put it on the man had to drape one corner over his left shoulder from back to front.

2. The other end was passed behind him, under his right arm, across his chest and back over his left shoulder. It was then pinned or tucked into place.

Hair

Roman women grew their hair long and liked to impress with elaborate hairstyles. Some dyed it, while others wore wigs. Blonde hair was especially fashionable. Romen men usually wore their hair short and were clean-shaven.

Jewellery and make-up

Women wore make-up to make their skin pale, and they loved wearing jewellery which was often made of gold and highly decorated.

Keeping clean

Romans took grooming seriously. Very few Romans had their own bathrooms so they visited the public baths. They would take their clothes off in the changing room and then go to the steam rooms to sweat. Romans didn't use soap. A slave would rub olive oil into the bather's skin and then scrape off the oil and dirt with a special curved tool called a strigil (left) before the bather took a refreshing dip in a cold pool. Men and women would use the baths at different times of day and enjoyed meeting friends there. Both men and women used perfume to keep them smelling sweet between visits to the baths.

A bronze strigil and glass oil flask dating from Roman times.

The Roman baths at Bath in the UK were built over a hot spring. They date from 60 CE.

Food and drink

Romans enjoyed sharing a meal with friends and family. The main meal of the day was dinner, which was generally eaten in the late afternoon.

Take-aways

Very few ordinary people had their own kitchen, so most people bought their hot food from one of the many local take-away food shops. Common foods included cheese, lentils, porridge, fruit and vegetables. Wealthy households had well-equipped kitchens where the cooking was done by slaves. They enjoyed a wide variety of spicy and exotic foods, often made with ingredients brought from abroad.

Part of a bread oven found in Pompeii.

Ordinary Romans ate from wooden plates and used bronze spoons like these.

Banquets

The Romans liked to give dinner parties or banquets. Diners sat or lay on couches around a low table while slaves served the many courses. Inviting a **guest of honour** made the party a particular success. Guests were expected to remove their shoes and slaves would wash the guests' feet, as well as their hands, as the Romans ate mainly with their fingers.

The Romans liked to impress their guests with exotic foods. Dishes could include boiled ostrich and roast flamingo!

How to enjoy the perfect Roman dinner party

Romans loved to give dinner parties and there were strict rules on how polite guests should behave. Sing this song as if you are a guest wanting to make a good impression.

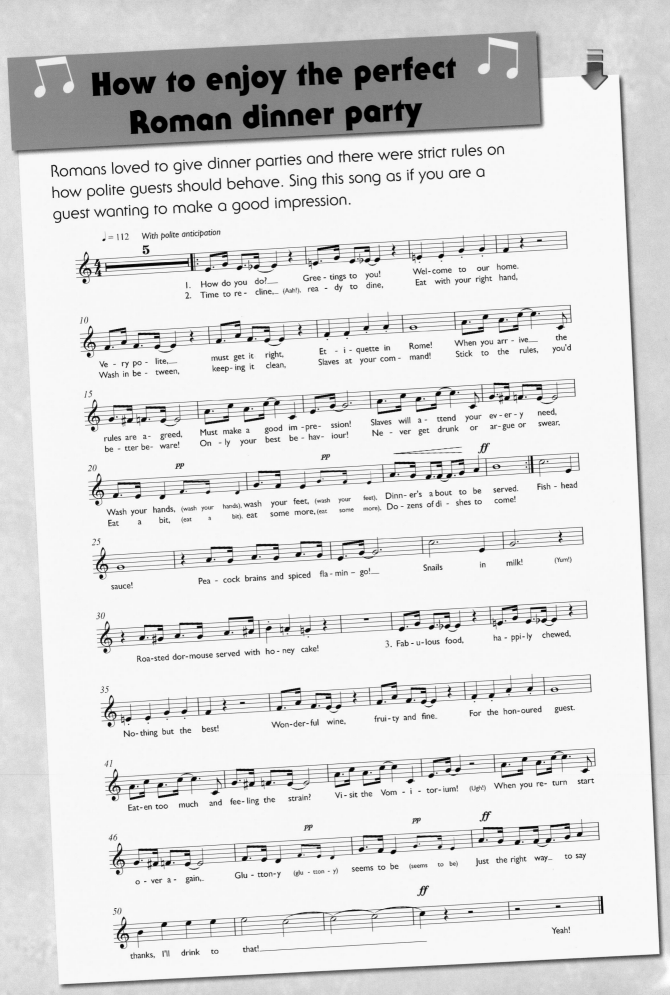

Fun and games

The Romans enjoyed all kinds of games and sports. They especially liked going to big public shows, such as plays, fights and races.

Out and about

The Romans built grand buildings for public entertainment across the empire. One of the most famous of all Roman buildings is the Colosseum in Rome. It was a huge arena where up to 50,000 people would gather to watch gladiators fight to the death, or wild animals fight each other. **Chariot** racing was also very popular.

Plays

Every large town had an open air theatre. Romans loved going to plays. All the actors were men and they wore masks to show what sort of **character** they were playing.

These men are acting out a Roman gladiator fight.

At home

It was very important for Romans to have a healthy body, and they enjoyed competitive sports and games such as athletics and wrestling.

At home, people played board and dice games which often involved betting on the result. It was common to see grids for games carved into floors of guardhouses, amphitheatres – wherever people might have time to have some fun!

A mosaic showing Roman men playing a board game.

Children's toys and games

Many of the toys that Roman children played with are still popular with children today. They included balls, hoops, dolls, model people and animals, marbles and toy chariots.

A toy chariot.

Tali

One game that was popular with both children and adults is still played today. We call it jacks or knucklebones.
The Romans called it tali, which was the name of the small knuckle or ankle bones of a sheep or goat that were used to play the game. You can make your own jacks as follows:

1. Roll a small piece of modelling clay into a ball about 1cm in diameter. Make four more balls to match.

2. Shape each ball into a short, fat cylinder.

3. Using your finger and thumb, press in both ends of each cylinder to make each piece look like a knucklebone (see above). Leave to dry.

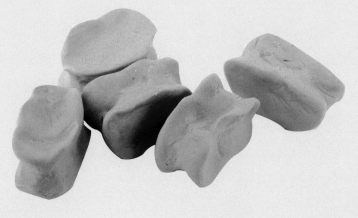

How to play: You can play tali in pairs or small groups.

- Play three or five rounds. Take it in turns to throw all five tali into the air and try to catch them on the back of your hand. Add up the number of tali caught in each round. The winner is the player with the biggest total caught.

Religion and beliefs

Religion played an important part in the life of most Romans. They believed it was very important to keep the gods happy.

Temples

The Romans built many fine temples across the Roman Empire to honour their gods. Only **priests** and **priestesses** could enter the temples. **Worshippers** who brought **offerings** for the god or goddess had to stay outside.

Jupiter

Juno

Great gods and goddesses

Jupiter: king of the gods

Juno: wife of Jupiter and goddess of women

Mars: god of war

Minerva: goddess of wisdom, crafts and trade

Neptune: god of the sea

Venus: goddess of love

Mercury: the messenger god

Diana: goddess of hunting

Vesta: goddess of the home and **hearth**

Vulcan: god of blacksmiths and volcanoes

Neptune

TRUE!

There was even a goddess of sewers named Cloacina.

At home

Every household had a **shrine** to worship the gods of the home. Every morning the head of the household would offer gifts and prayers to the gods to protect the family against thieves and evil spirits.

Superstition

The Romans were very **superstitious**. Before starting a journey or project they would consult a **soothsayer** for their advice. According to legend, the emperor Julius Caesar (see page 20) was murdered after he ignored a soothsayer's advice to stay at home.

Shrines to the household gods were an important part of every Roman home.

Make a golden snake armband

The Romans wore jewellery and other items like this snake armband because they believed they would protect them from bad luck.

1. Draw a long snake (55 cm x 1.5 cm) onto a piece of thin gold card. Cut out the shape.

2. Draw round the first shape onto another piece of gold card and cut out the shape.

3. Glue or tape a piece of thin wire onto the back of one shape.

4. Glue the second shape on top of the first, matching up the edges. Leave to dry. Draw on eyes with a marker pen. Bend the snake into a spiral to fit round your arm.

Beware the Ides of March

In Roman times the middle day of any month was known as the Ides. The murder of the Roman ruler Julius Caesar on the 15th of March, 44 BCE was a very important and shocking event in Roman history. Sing this song as though you have just heard the dreadful news and are discussing it with your family and friends.

♩ = 106   *Agitated*

1. Be - ware the Ides of March, the dread - ed Ides of
   ware the Ides of March, the dread - ed Ides of

March! How could a nor - mal day, an ord - in - ar - y day Turn in - to such a cat - a - stro -
March! When he ig - nored ad - vice he had to pay the price, He should have list - ened to what was

phe? Be - ware the Ides of March, the dread - ed Ides of March! A sun - ny
said! Be - ware the Ides of March, the dread - ed Ides of March! The sit - u -

day in Spring, no fear of an - y - thing, That end - ed up as a tra - ge - dy!
a - tion's grim 'cos peo - ple hat - ed him And ma - ny want - ed to see him dead!

Ju - lius Cae - sar set out for the Sen - ate ve - ry near, Met a man who told him this was
O - ver at the Sen - ate things weren't happ - en - ing as planned, Cae - sar was surr - ound - ed by a

not a good i - dea! Warned him not to go, he said the dan - ger would be great,
mean and moo - dy band, Stabbed him one by one, the men he used to call his friends,

1.
Stay at home and a - void an aw - ful fate.
Cae - sar fell, and his life was at an end!

2. Be

2.
Be - ware! Be - ware! Be - ware!

End of the empire

By the 4th century CE ways of life in the Roman Empire were changing, and its very existence was coming under attack.

Christianity

Towards the end of Roman rule, **Christianity** became the main religion in the empire. Early Christians had been **persecuted** for their beliefs and even thrown to the lions and other wild animals as part of the entertainment in public shows. However after the Roman Emperor Constantine I (306-337 CE) became a Christian in 324 CE, Christianity quickly spread to many parts of the empire.

A Roman coin showing the head of the first Christian emperor, Constantine I.

Rome falls

In the third century CE the great Roman Empire began to break up. It was already ruled by two different emperors, one in the east, the other in the west. As the empire got bigger, it became more and more difficult to defend its borders and to keep order. Rome itself began to come under attack from armies from the north known as Barbarians. By the end of the fifth century CE a group called the Goths had completely conquered Rome and its surrounding areas, forcing the last western Roman emperor, Romulus Augustus, to flee the city.

TRUE!
At its height, the Roman Empire covered over three million kilometres of Asia, Europe and Africa.

Romulus Augustus (right) surrenders Rome to Odoacer (on horseback), leader of the Goths.

How do we know?

We know a lot about Rome and Roman **civilisation** because they left so many things behind, scattered across their great empire.

Buildings

Many spectacular Roman ruins still exist, some in Rome, but others as far afield as Turkey and North Africa. Some buildings, such as the Pantheon in Rome, with its striking **domed** roof, are still in use today. Other ruins, such as the fort of Vindolanda on Hadrian's Wall in northern England, and the great aqueduct at Nîmes in France (see page 8) have taught **historians** much about the engineering the Romans used.

The ruins of this Roman amphitheatre are found in El Djem in Tunisia.

Roads

Roman roads were so well built that stretches of them still exist. A saying tells us that 'all roads lead to Rome', and it was true that Roman roads allowed easy travel between Rome and the rest of the empire. They were built of several layers of earth, gravel and loose stones and topped with paving stones. The top was curved to allow water to drain off into ditches dug on either side. They were also built in straight lines.

The Via Appia led straight from the south of Italy to the heart of Rome.

The volcano Mount Vesuvius looms behind the ruins of the ancient city of Pompeii.

Buried treasure

In 79 BCE the volcano Mount Vesuvius **erupted** and the nearby cities of Pompeii and Herculaneum were buried under several metres of choking, burning dust. When **archaeologists** dug down to uncover the ruins, they found whole streets completely **preserved**, with homes, shops and even people and animals still lying where they fell when the volcano erupted. This has given historians lots of very valuable information about how the Romans lived.

This Roman mosaic warns visitors to 'Cave canem' or 'Beware of the dog!'

TRUE!

Romans wrote graffiti on walls to say how they felt about people or events.

Writing and pictures

Romans wrote and spoke in Latin, a language that is still understood today. Many documents and carvings still survive, as do Roman paintings and mosaics on walls and floors of buildings. All of these help historians to understand the greatest empire there has ever been.

CAVE CANEM

The Roman legacy

The Roman civilisation had a great influence on the rest of the world, particularly across Europe.

Engineering

There are buildings all over the world constructed in the Roman style. Two particularly well known examples are the Capitol building and the White House in Washington D.C., USA, which were built to look like Roman temples. Many roads across Europe still follow the straight tracks of the first Roman roads, and much of our modern town planning is based on the Roman grid system.

The Capitol building in Washington D.C.

Inventions

The Romans gave us many inventions which are still part of everyday life. These include central heating, plumbing, socks, candles, calendars and glass windows.

Language

The Roman **script** is the one that is most widely used across the world today. Latin is the basis of several European languages – French, Spanish, Portuguese and Romanian – and thousands of words used in English are taken from Latin, including the scientific names for plants and animals.

This page is from the Gutenberg Bible. It was written in Latin and printed in Germany around 1455.

TRUE!

Many people today have Roman names. These include Amanda, Antony, Diana, Laura, Marcus, Martin, Patricia, Julia and Virginia.

What did the Romans do for us?

The Romans were great inventors and the way they lived their lives has had a huge influence on the modern world. Sing this song to celebrate those inventions which have improved our lives today.

Beware the Ides of March

When a Roman boy celebrated his 14th birthday, he was considered to become a man and was given his first adult toga. It was a very important rite of passage for a young Roman.

Cast

- **Severus**, *an elderly slave, steward of the household*
- **Galla**, *a slave girl*
- **Paulina**, *a slave*
- **Marcus**, *aged 14, son of Drusilla and Gaius*
- **Lucius**, *aged 9, brother of Marcus*
- **Claudia**, *aged 12, sister of Marcus*
- **Drusilla**, *wife of Gaius and mother of the children*
- **Gaius**, *a government official and father of the children*
- **Titus Horatius Aquila**, *senator (say Horayshius Akweela)*

Props

- *Set of tali (jacks)*
- *Cups of drinks on trays for slaves to hand to the guests*
- *Bulla*
- *Plain white toga for Marcus*
- *Rolled paper (letter of freedom)*
- *Roman style costumes and a senator's toga with purple edging for Titus*

SONG 1   *'Civis Romanus Sum'*

Severus: *(Enters and speaks to the audience)* Good afternoon, ladies and gentlemen. My name is Severus. I'm one of the family slaves here, steward of the household and at your service. *(He bows)* Today is a very special day. It's the master Marcus's fourteenth birthday, the day he comes of age, so his father and mother are giving a banquet to celebrate. We were up before daybreak preparing.

(Enter Galla looking nervous at being in the front part of the house)

Severus   What are you doing here, Galla?

Galla: My lady told me to come and wait for the boys returning from school so I could tell Master Marcus to hurry and get himself ready.

Severus: Right. Well as soon as you have done that you need to get back to the kitchen. The guests will be arriving very soon and we still have things to carry into the dining room. *(Galla goes to stand by the front door)*

Severus   *(Turns back to talk to the audience again)* We're very lucky here, unlike a lot of family slaves I know! Our master's a good man, treats us well, just like his father did before him. I've been here nearly all my life, ever since I was a small boy and my mother and I were sold for slaves after my father was killed in battle. *(Enter Paulina)*

Paulina: Can you come, please, Severus, you're needed in the kitchen.

Severus: Just coming. *(To audience)* Can't stand here gossiping! There's a very special guest coming today, Senator Titus Horatius Aquila. He's a very important man and it's a big honour for the family so my lady wants everything to be just right.

(Exit Severus into the house as Marcus and Lucius come in from outside. Lucius gets out his tali and starts playing on the floor)

Marcus: That's it! No more school, ever!

Lucius: It's not fair! It's so boring, and I'm fed up of getting beaten by the teacher all the time for no reason.

Marcus: Well maybe you should try working harder instead of messing about with your friends all the time. Hello Galla, what is it?

Galla: Your mother says please will you go and get ready for your guests.

Marcus: All right. *(Teasing his brother as Galla exits)* See, I'm a man now!

(He sits down and starts playing with Lucius as Claudia comes in)

Claudia: Hello, boys.

Marcus: Hello Claudia, how has your day been?

Claudia: Boring as usual! Mother says you've got to come and get ready.

Marcus: *(Not moving)* All right, I'm coming.

Claudia: I wish I could come to school with you.

Lucius: You wouldn't if you did! Anyway you're supposed to be learning how to be a good wife. Mind you, I can't think why anyone would want to marry you!

Claudia: *(Lunging towards him)* Shut up or I'll hit you!

(They start a mock fight as Drusilla comes in, very cross)

Drusilla: Children! What on earth is going on? Claudia stop that at once! That's no way for a young lady to behave. Marcus, what are you still doing here? You're supposed to be getting ready. This party's all for you, you know. The guests will be arriving any minute now.

Marcus: *(Getting up quickly)* Sorry, Mother.

Drusilla: Did you go to the bathhouse on the way home like I told you to?

Marcus: Yes, Mother.

Drusilla: Good. Oh and have any of you seen your father?

Children: No, Mother.

(Children go out as their father comes hurrying in)

Gaius: Sorry I'm late, my dear.

Drusilla: Wherever have you been? Our guests will be arriving in a minute! And Titus Horatius Aquila as well, we must be ready for him.

Gaius: Well I hope he's still able to come. There's a very strange atmosphere around the city today, lots of rumours. I'm not sure what's going on, but something's not right. Maybe he'll know more if and when he gets here but I think we may need to start without him.

SONG 2: 'Roman Etiquette'

(During the song guests arrive and are ushered in by Severus, greeted by Gaius, Drusilla and Marcus and offered drinks by Paulina and Galla)

Gaius: My friends, welcome, and thank you for coming here today to help us celebrate the birthday of our son Marcus and his coming of age as a citizen of Rome. *(Applause, calls of 'Congratulations' from guests)* We are hoping that our friend Titus Horatius Aquila will be able to join us but he may be late so we will start the ceremony without him. Marcus? You know what to do.

(Marcus steps forward and removes the bulla that he has been wearing round his neck since he was a baby)

Marcus: As I put aside this bulla, a sign of childhood no longer needed, I pray that the gods will give me strength to live my life as a man with honour, wisdom and justice.

Gaius: Drusilla, the toga please. *(Drusilla hands him the new toga and he helps his son to wrap it around himself)* May the gods bring you good fortune. *(The guests repeat 'May the gods bring you good fortune')* And now let us go into the dining room to eat.

(As the guests start to move, Titus comes in, clearly upset)

Gaius: Titus Aquila, welcome. We are honoured to greet you.

Titus: I fear you may not be so pleased to see me when you hear the bad news I bring. Julius Caesar, our noble ruler, has been murdered! He was stabbed this afternoon by a group of senators whom he believed were his friends. Apparently he was warned by a soothsayer not to go to the Senate at all today. 'Beware the Ides of March' is what he was apparently told, but he took no notice. The city is in a state of panic!

SONG 3: **'Beware the Ides of March!'**

Guest: *(Horrified)* Who has done this dreadful thing and why?

Guest: And what will happen now?

Titus: The army has been ordered onto the streets to keep the peace and to guard against any rioting. I was in the building nearby and heard a lot of shouting. I went down with some other people to see what was happening, but there were soldiers everywhere and we couldn't get near. Then word began to spread that the killers included people like Gaius Cassius and Marcus Brutus.

Gaius: But they are his friends, honourable men.

Titus: Well, apparently they believed Julius Caesar was about to declare himself king. And that of course would be very dangerous. But I fear that Rome is now facing a very unsettled time as there is no clear candidate to replace him.

Drusilla: Oh dear, and on such a happy day for us. Now everybody will remember the Ides of March for all the wrong reasons!

Titus: I know, and I do apologise, young man, for spoiling your special day.

Marcus: No Sir, it's not your fault, and thank you for still coming.

Titus: Spoken like a true Roman, Marcus. And Rome will survive this crisis because we are strong. History will remember this day forever as the beginning of a new era.

Gaius: Well said, Titus. And I would like to mark this day as the beginning of a new era for our son by showing him how being a Roman citizen also means being just and compassionate. We have a slave called Severus who by chance came to us on this very day as a young boy. He has served us faithfully all these years and deserves the chance to enjoy an honourable retirement. I have therefore decided to give him his freedom. Severus, please step forward. *(Hands him a rolled paper)* You are now a free man, free to stay with us or go wherever you wish. The choice is yours.

Severus: *(In a state of shock)* I don't know what to say, Master. Thank you.

Gaius: I am not your master any more. You will receive a sum of money to start your new life as a free man, part of the greatest city on Earth, and may the gods bring you good fortune.

SONG 4: **'What did the Romans do for us?'**

Glossary

archaeologist - someone who digs up objects to find out about the past

barracks - a building where soldiers live

ceremony - a special occasion, such as a wedding or funeral

character - a person in a play or film

chariot - a two-wheeled vehicle which was drawn by horses

charm - an object that is believed to be lucky

Christianity - a religion that follows the teachings of Jesus Christ

citizen - in Rome, someone who had rights and freedoms that others were not allowed, such as the right to vote in elections

civilisation - a group of people with their own organisation and culture

conquer - to defeat (in battle)

domed - shaped like a semi-circle

durable - long-lasting

election - when people vote for a person to take power

empire - all the land under the control of a race of people

engineer - someone who designs and helps construct buildings and structures

erupt - when a volcano throws out hot rocks, lava and ash

fort - a place that can be defended

gladiators - men who fought in arenas to entertain people

guest of honour - an especially important guest

hearth - a fireplace

historian - someone who studies the past

inhabitants - the people who live in a place

legend - an old story

linen - a tough cloth woven from flax

motto - a short saying

offerings - gifts, such as food or money, that were offered to the gods to keep them happy

pension - money paid to people when they stop working

persecute - to treat someone badly, for example because of their religion or race

preserve - to stop something from ageing

priest/ess - a holy person

prisoners of war - people who are taken prisoner by the enemy during war

rights - things that every person should have, such as the right to speak freely

script - any type of writing

senators - powerful men who made the laws

shrine - a place where people can worship a god

soothsayer - someone who claimed to be able to see into the future

standard - a long pole with badges or flags on it that was carried by a Roman soldier

superstitious - someone who believes in things that have no basis in truth, such as that the number 13 is unlucky

taxes - money paid to the government

toga - a piece of cloth that was draped around the body

tribe - a group of people of a particular descent and culture who live in the same place

tunic - a sleeveless, knee-length item of clothing

worshipper - someone who gives thanks and prays to a god

Index

Find out more

http://www.bbc.co.uk/schools/
primaryhistory/romans/
A fun educational site exploring lots of
aspects of Roman life. Includes games
and a timeline.

http://rome.mrdonn.org
Lots of information on the Roman
civilisation, particularly on ways of
life. Includes games, craft activities
and maps.

Note to parents and teachers: every effort has
been made by the Publishers to ensure that these
websites are suitable for children, that they are of
the highest educational value, and that they contain
no inappropriate or offensive material. However,
because of the nature of the Internet, it is impossible
to guarantee that the contents of these sites will not
be altered. We strongly advise that Internet access is
supervised by a responsible adult.